Reading Essentials in Social Studies

THE ANCIENT WORLD

CHINA

STEPHEN HANKS AND JARRETT A. LOBELL

Perfection Learning®

About the Authors

Stephen Hanks wrote many articles about the ancient world as the founding editor in chief of *DIG* magazine between 1999 and 2001. Stephen has edited many other magazines, including *Scholastic News, Major League Baseball for Kids, KidSports,* and *New York Sports.* As a writer, his articles have appeared in *Esquire, SPORT* magazine, the *New York Daily News, Newsday*, and many others. He and his family live in Brooklyn, New York.

Jarrett A. Lobell is an archaeologist and writer who has worked for many years on sites all over the world. For seven years, she was the director of an archaeological field school in Pompeii, Italy, and taught hundreds of students from over 25 different countries about the fascinating field of archaeology. Jarrett is also the photography editor for *Archaeology* magazine. After living in many other places, including Rome, Athens, and Pompeii, Jarrett has come home to New York City to live ... at least for the time being.

PHOTO CREDITS: Cover: Corel, www.arttoday.com; 4,5—www.arttoday.com; 6,7—Private Collection/Bridgeman Art Library; 8—British Museum, London, UK/Bridgeman Art Library (top), Zhang Shui Cheng/Bridgeman Art Library (bottom); 9—Private Collection/Bridgeman Art Library; 10—British Library, London, UK/Bridgeman Art Library; 11—Oriental Bronzes Ltd, London, UK/Bridgeman Art Library (left) Paul Macapia (right); 12—Private Collection/Bridgeman Art Library (top), Private Collection/Bridgeman Art Library (bottom); 13—Bibliotheque Nationale, Paris, France/Bridgeman Art Library (top), Victoria & Albert Museum, London, UK/Bridgeman Art Library (bottom); 14, 15—Private Collection/The Stapleton Collection/Bridgeman Art Library; 16—Private Collection/The Stapleton Collection/Bridgeman Art Library; 18—Oriental Museum, Durham University, UK/Bridgeman Art Library (top), Freer Gallery, Smithsonian Institution, Washington, USA/Bridgeman Art Library (bottom); 19—Chengdu, Sichuan Province, China/Roger-Viollet, Paris/Bridgeman Art Library; 20, 21—Christie's Images, London, UK/Bridgeman Art Library; 22—www.arttoday.com; 24—National Museums of Scotland/Bridgeman Art Library; 25—www.arttoday.com; 26—Bibliotheque Nationale, Paris, France/Archives Charmet/Bridgeman Art Library; 27—www.arttoday.com (3); 28–33—Tomb of Qin shi Huang Di, Xianyang, China/Bridgeman Art Library; 34, 35—Courtesy World Monuments Fund; 36—www.arttoday.com; 38—Courtesy World Monuments Fund; 39—Courtesy NASA (top), World Monuments Fund (bottom); 40, 41—Private Collection/The Stapleton Collection/Bridgeman Art Library; 42—www.arttoday.com (top), Private Collection/The Stapleton Collection/Bridgeman Art Library (bottom); 43—Peel Antiques, London, UK/Bridgeman Art Library; 44—www.arttoday.com (2); 45—Private Collection/Bridgeman Art Library (left), British Museum, London, UK/Bridgeman Art Library (right); 46—Forbidden City, Beijing, China/Ali Meyer/Bridgeman Art Library.

Designer: Ken Feisel Photo Editor: Jarrett A. Lobell

For information, contact
Perfection Learning® Corporation,
1000 North Second Avenue,
P.O. Box 500, Logan, Iowa 51546-0500
Tel: 1-800-831-4190 • Fax 1-800-543-2745
perfectionlearning.com

4549 20042 8

3 4 5 6 7 PP 08 07 06 05 04

ISBN 0-7569-4185-7

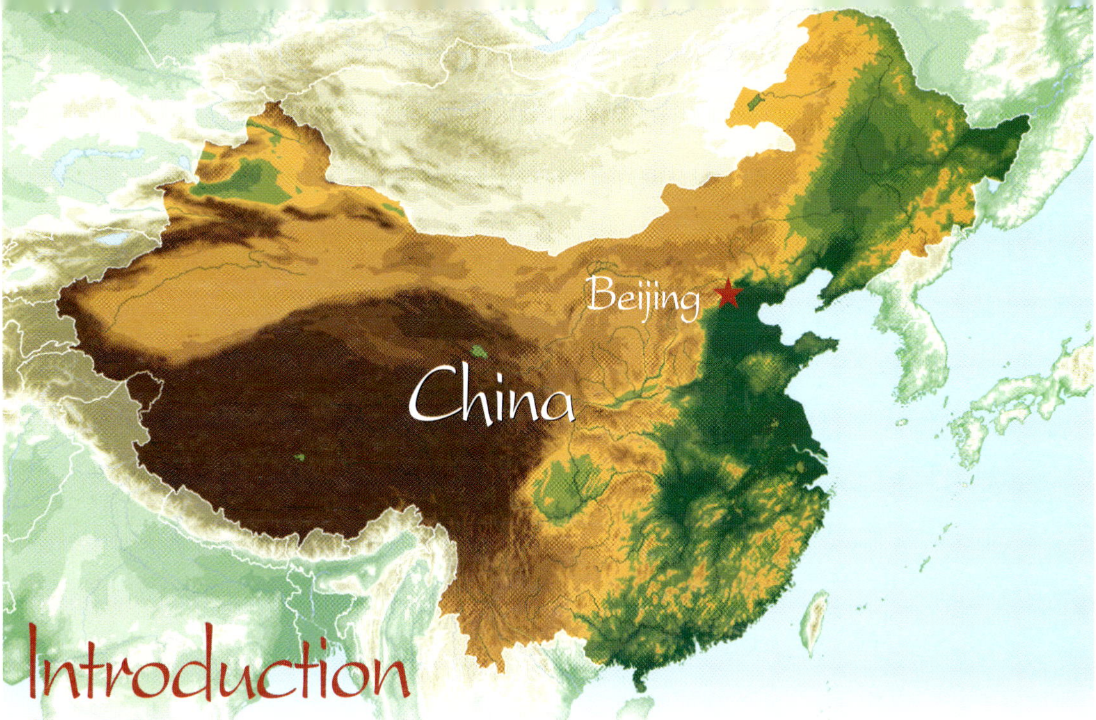

Introduction

People have been living in the area we call China for more than 50,000 years. In fact, some of the earliest human remains have been found in China. In 1967, Peking Man, one of the most famous fossils of prehistoric human beings to be found anywhere in the world, was discovered in Choukoutien, southwest of Beijing. Chinese civilization advanced over many thousands of years—through wars, famine, and many families of emperors called **dynasties**. During this time, there were great moments of invention, discovery, and exploration. Read on for a whirlwind tour of 3,500 years of Chinese history.

Table of Contents

Timeline of Important Events in

Spinning silk

1766 B.C. The Shang dynasty, the second dynasty in ancient China, flourishes along the banks of the Yellow River and ends around 1027 B.C.

1384 B.C. P'an Keng founds the city of Anyang. By this time, Chinese culture has developed both writing and art.

Lao-tzu

1300 B.C. The Chinese invent silk.

1027 B.C. The last Shang ruler, Chou Hsin, is conquered by Wu-wang, and the Chou dynasty begins. It lasts until 221 B.C., longer than any other dynasty in China. It is typically divided into three periods.

- the Western Chou period (1027–771 B.C.)
- the Ch'un Ch'iu period (722–481 B.C.)
- the Warring States period (481–221 B.C.)

A statue of Buddha

600–500 B.C. Lao-tzu, author of *The Tao Te Ching* and founder of **Taoism**, lives around this time. He encourages people to live simply and according to nature.

563 B.C. Prince Siddhartha Gautama, the founder of **Buddhism**, is born in India.

the History of Ancient China

Confucius

The Great Wall

A porcelain teapot

551 B.C.	K'ung Fu-tzu (Confucius) is born. He teaches the importance of centralized authority and piety. Like Aristotle, he believes the state to be a natural institution.
481 B.C.	The Warring States period begins. A class structure emerges consisting of the lesser nobility (including scholars), the peasant farmers, the **artisans**, and the merchants—who hold the lowest position in society.
479 B.C.	The philosopher Mo-tzu, founder of **Mohism**, is born. He teaches a message of universal love and compassion for the common plight of ordinary people.
221 B.C.	The Qin emerge as victors at the end of the Warring States period. Prince Qin Shihuangdi names himself the first Qin emperor and begins unifying China.
214 B.C.	Great Wall of China construction begins.
207 B.C.	The Qin dynasty ends.
105 A.D.	The Chinese invent paper.
264–273 A.D.	The Chinese invent tea.
800 A.D.	The Chinese invent gunpowder.

爱

CHAPTER I

The History of

The first solid archaeological evidence of a Chinese civilization comes at the time of the Shang dynasty (1766 B.C.). During this period, the Chinese people lived under a king who was also the head priest. These ancient people built walled cities, left written records, and used chariots for transportation and warfare. The Shang also practiced human sacrifice. When a Shang king died, many of his slaves were beheaded or buried alive with him.

Ancient China

The next powerful dynasty in China was the Chou, a group of **nomads** who overthrew the Shang and ruled China from 1027–221 B.C. In this period, kings became less powerful and established a **feudal state**. The kings chose local nobles to rule over parcels of land and the people on them. This created a great deal of loyalty between the rulers, the nobles, and the families who farmed the land. The Chou rulers used the money they earned from taxes to build roads, **irrigation** systems, and good walls around their cities to encourage farming.

A 14th-century painting on silk showing a convoy of Mongols

The famous Chinese philosopher Confucius also lived during this time (551–479 B.C.). Confucius was a great man who developed a code of ethics that was based on the goodness of the human spirit. Soon, however, Chinese society entered a violent period called the Time of the Warring States (481–221 B.C.), when cities became more powerful and took the place of the old system of feudal landlords.

The First Emperors

At the end of the Time of the Warring States, the Qin state emerged victorious. So in 221 B.C., China was united under the Qin dynasty. Although this dynasty lasted only 15 years, it greatly influenced the future of Chinese history. Qin emperors, especially Qui Shihuangdi who was China's first emperor, established a centralized government and a standard system of weights, measures, and writing that was used throughout the country. During this period, construction of the Great Wall of China began. It is also from the Qin dynasty that we get the name China.

Above: Bronze vessel made during the Shang dynasty, more than 3,000 years ago. Below: Bronze pot from Western China, 1027–256 B.C.

Follow the Yellow Silk Road

Before the explorer Vasco de Gama's discovery of the sea route from Europe to India in the 15th century, the Silk Road was the most important trade route in the world. For almost 1,600 years, the Silk Road functioned as the superhighway of its time, carrying all kinds of goods, ideas, and technology from the East to the West and back.

The Silk Road was not just a single road but a 4,000-mile long route from eastern China all the way to the Mediterranean Sea. The route was dangerous and ran across desolate deserts and over massive mountains. All along the way, Chinese merchants exchanged silk, tea, furs, and spices for gold, silver, precious stones, glass, ivory, horses, and wool.

The history of the Silk Road follows the history of China. At stable times, such as during the Han and Tang dynasties, commerce along the Silk Road flourished. During times of war, trade was difficult and disrupted. This remarkable route was not called the Silk Road until the mid-19th century when German geographer Baron Ferdinand von Richtofen coined this romantic term. The name recalls the fact that although silk was not the only item traded on the route, it was often the most popular one.

Terra-cotta camel and servant, Tang dynasty (618–906 A.D.). Camels were used to travel along the difficult terrain of the Silk Road.

Detail of an atlas from 1375 showing Marco Polo and his family traveling by camel caravan

Amazing Traveler

Marco Polo was born in 1254 A.D. and lived in the Italian city of Venice. The son of a noble family, Marco was well educated and dreamed of the far-off places he read about in his studies. When he was just 17 years old, Marco and his family began a 24-year-long trip along the ancient Silk Road that was one of the most remarkable journeys of all time. He traveled from Italy to China through Armenia, Persia, and Afghanistan.

In May 1275, the Polos arrived at the Mongol capital of Beijing and were greeted by the emperor Kublai Khan. It had been three and a half years since they left Venice, and they had traveled a total of 5,600 miles. Needing a rest, Marco and his family stayed in Kublai Khan's court for 17 years, acquiring great wealth as well as knowledge of the incredible inventions of the Chinese.

When it was finally time for Marco to return home, his sea voyage lasted two years, during which most of his crew died from disease and piracy. Once back in Venice, Marco Polo published his *Description of the World*, or *The Travels of Marco Polo*, amazing the world with the wonders he had seen along the Silk Road. Many people did not believe the tales Marco told—they were just too astounding to comprehend. Although Marco had traveled far and seen incredible things, his famous last words were "I did not even tell half of what I saw."

The Han dynasty followed the Qin and ruled China from 206 B.C.–220 A.D. Early on, the biggest threat to the Han came from the **Huns**, nomadic tribes who originated in north-central Asia. The Emperor Wu Ti (140–87 B.C.) finally beat the Huns and established important trade routes, including the famous Silk Road.

The last Han emperor was forced to resign after a popular uprising called the Rebellion of the Yellow Turbans. Several hundred years of chaos followed until the Emperor Weng, the first emperor of the Sui dynasty (580–618 A.D.), was able to reunite the country.

A horse and his groom made of bronze from the Eastern Han dynasty (1st–3rd century A.D.)

The Sui emperors introduced a system of electing officials that remained in use until the 20th century. These emperors also built the Imperial (Great) Canal, a huge engineering project to join China's three major rivers. The last Sui emperor, Yang Ti, was assassinated and replaced by one of his army's officers, Li Shih Min, the founder of the Tang dynasty.

Under the Tang emperors (618–907 A.D.), Chinese culture blossomed. At least 50,000 poems by more than 2,000 poets and many paintings and sculptures survive from this period.

A pottery fishmonger found in a tomb from the Han dynasty

But soon the Tang dynasty declined and another period of war and struggle for power, called the Period of Five Dynasties, affected China. Barbarian warlords ruled the northern part of China and the south was split into ten different kingdoms.

Peace finally came under the Song dynasty (960–1277 A.D.), and China again flourished. During this dynasty, many great Chinese inventions were perfected, including gunpowder, printing, and **porcelain**.

From 1211 to 1258 A.D., much of China was attacked by a powerful and fearsome group of warriors called the

Colorful Tang dynasty (618–906 A.D.) terra-cotta figurines of a camel, brightly dressed guardian figures standing on bulls and a horse and his groom

A 14th-century French manuscript shows the Chinese emperor Kublai Khan (1214–1294 A.D.) giving his golden seal to the Polos upon their arrival in his new capital of Cambaluc.

Mongols led by the king Genghis Khan and later his grandson Kublai Khan. The Mongols conquered the Chinese in 1278 A.D., and Kublai Khan became the emperor. He established the Yuan dynasty and ruled over an enormous empire. With a stable economy and with Beijing the center of trade in **Eurasia**, Chinese trade in porcelain and spices again flourished. In 1325 A.D., however, a famine devastated the Chinese empire, and as many as 8 million people died. The people blamed the Mongols for the famine, eventually driving them out in 1368 A.D. and establishing the Ming dynasty, which ruled China for the next 300 years.

爱

CHAPTER II

Daily Life in Ancient China

A 19th-century engraving showing the process of drying, dying, and winding silk

For thousands of years, the people of ancient China lived off the land, supporting themselves by growing many different crops and raising animals. The earliest traces of agriculture and domestication of animals in China date as far back as 8000 B.C. At this time, people used stone tools, lived mostly in caves, used fire for warmth and cooking, and probably had some simple ways of speaking and communicating.

Over thousands of years, these basic skills developed and ancient Chinese society grew up around peasants who farmed small pieces of land. Every member of the family worked the land, dug the ditches necessary for irrigation, or helped to cut the **terraces** into the hillsides that made farming a mountainous country like China possible.

Farming and Food

In the northern part of China, farmers grew mostly wheat; barley; and millet, a type of grain. In the south, they grew mostly rice. The ancient farmers grew crops for themselves and to supply the army and the cities with food. China's ancient farmers also raised pigs and chickens and used oxen and buffalo to pull their carts and plows.

As in all ancient cultures, the Chinese diet depended on a person's economic position. Poor people ate simple meals consisting mainly of rice, grains, some vegetables, and beans. Occasionally, they ate chicken or a wild bird or fish they had caught. Wealthy people's diets were much more varied and included pork, lamb, duck, goose, pigeon, and venison (deer), as well as many different kinds of fresh fruits and vegetables.

On special occasions, the wealthy Chinese people even ate snakes, snails, sparrows, and bear claws. Both rich and poor people used spices, honey, and soy sauce to flavor their food. Usually food was cut up into small pieces and either steamed or cooked quickly in a wok, a deep iron frying pan. People drank tea, water, or a kind of wine made from fermented rice.

Chinese peasants are shown plowing the land in a 17th-century Dutch engraving. From the 13th century on, travelers from all over Europe came to China and recorded what they saw in books and drawings.

Clothing and Housing

Like food, differences in clothing also distinguished rich from poor in ancient China. Peasants usually wore a long shirt of woven hemp, a rough fabric made from locally grown plant fibers. They wore little or no jewelry and only crude sandals on their feet. Wealthy people, however, wore clothing made of fine silks and jewelry made from gold, jade, and other semiprecious stones. Men almost always wore a hat in public. Women arranged their hair in topknots fastened with fancy hairpins and wore elaborate makeup. Beginning in the Sui dynasty (581–618 A.D.), only the emperor was allowed to wear the color yellow.

Most ancient Chinese homes were built of mud bricks with roofs made of either reeds or tiles. In order to keep warmer in the winter and cooler in the summer, the floors of the houses were sunken into the earth and below ground level. Poor people would usually cook outside and share a communal toilet and bath. Wealthier homes had their own private kitchens and bathrooms.

Whether rich or poor, many generations lived in the home together and family pride and honor was the bond that held Chinese society together for thousands of years. The oldest male was the head of the household, and men were thought to be superior to women. Only sons could go to school or inherit property.

A favorite ancient Chinese game is called a *tangram*, which is a square cut into seven pieces, then reassembled into hundreds of different shapes. Trace and cut out the tangram below, then see if you can fit the pieces together to match the patterns shown—or make up your own.

Entertainment

The ancient Chinese loved games and sports. They played chess, card games, and board games. One 5th-century board game, called *wei-ch'i*, was a complex strategy game played on a chesslike grid of lines and boxes. Wealthy Chinese also hunted, wrote poetry, and grew extraordinary miniature trees called *bonsai*.

A terra-cotta figurine, from a Tang dynasty (618–907 A.D.) tomb, of a woman playing polo

Performances of all kinds were popular throughout Chinese history, and people often went to theater, magic, and acrobatic shows; martial arts displays; dances; and concerts. Favorite sports were wrestling, kite flying, badminton, and a game similar to Frisbee. Both kite flying and badminton were invented in China.

Writing

The oldest Chinese writings are the Oracle Bone inscriptions, extraordinary early examples from the Shang dynasty (around 1200 B.C.). The Oracle Bones are a group of inscriptions on fossilized animal bones and tortoise shells found near the last Shang capital of Anyang. These inscriptions contain ancient remedies for all kinds of sicknesses and records of the Chinese calendar.

A Yuan dynasty (1269–1368 A.D.) manuscript on paper mounted on silk showing the beauty not only of Chinese painting, but also of Chinese calligraphy

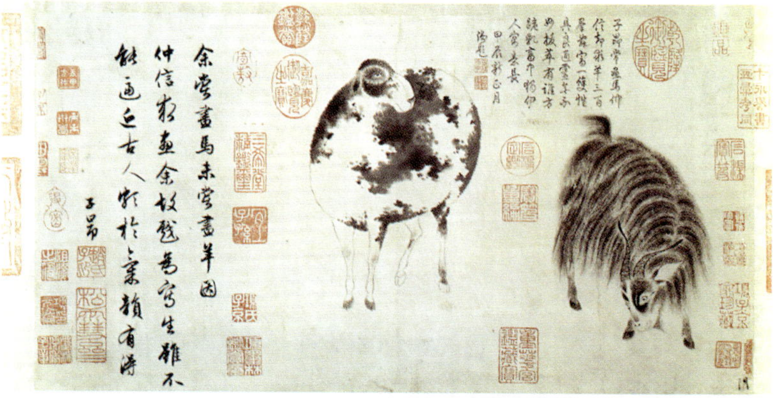

The Oracle Bones were named for their part in the ancient Chinese practice of **divination**. Other examples of ancient Chinese writing include inscriptions on bronze vessels and tablets, usually used in religious rituals. Beginning in about the 5th century B.C., the Chinese began writing on bamboo strips using a brush, wooden tablets, and silk cloth. These documents record rituals and remedies, as well as philosophy, poetry, and history. Classical Chinese, the language used in these writings, remained largely the same for more than 2,000 years until the 19th century.

Unlike English, the Chinese language is written in characters instead of letters. Letters are single forms that represent the sound of spoken language, whereas characters are complex forms that represent ideas, multiple sounds, or even pictures of the word. The character is composed of strokes, each of which has its own significance.

Are You a Rat?

The calendar was very important to the Chinese. Legend has it that the Emperor Shihuangdi invented the calendar based on the phases of the moon. Each year had 12 months of 29 1/2 days each, and a year of 365 days, which accounts for leap years consisting of 13 months. The years themselves went through a cycle of twelve as well, with each year named after one of the animals in the Chinese zodiac: dog, tiger, dragon, snake, horse, rat, pig, rabbit, ox, rooster, monkey, and goat. It was believed that you inherited personality traits from the animal whose sign you were born under.

Animal signs of the Chinese zodiac surround the symbol of Yin and Yang on a large stone disc from a temple in Chendu, Sichuan Province.

爱

CHAPTER III

Religion of Ancient China

An ivory Buddha sits on a throne made of turquoise in this marvelous Ming dynasty (1368–1644 A.D.) figurine.

There are five major religions or philosophies observed in China today, all of which had their beginnings in ancient Chinese society. Two of these, **Confucianism** and Taoism, were developed in China, while the others—Buddhism, Islam, and Christianity—all came to China from the outside. Both Confucianism and Taoism are philosophies that provide guidelines for ethical and proper individual behavior. Buddhism, Christianity, and Islam are more conventional religions based on the regular practice of rituals and the gathering of followers in a place of worship.

Confucianism

The philosopher Confucius, the founder of Confucianism, was born in northeastern China in 551 B.C. At this time, many small kingdoms were at war with one another, and Chinese society was in upheaval. Growing up in this violent environment, Confucius believed peace in China depended on a good and stable government with fair and just leaders. Confucius taught that people should have love for one another and for nature and treat both with kindness and care. This concept is called *jen*.

Confucius also taught that leaders should earn their jobs through education and talent, not through family connections or wealth, and that society must respect laws. For Confucius, society was based on a rigid system of relationships—ruler and ruled, husband and wife, parents and children, older and younger brothers, and between friends.

Confucius left a powerful **legacy** in his own writings and through his students who collected his teachings after his death. Soon many of the rules of Chinese society and education were based on Confucianism, which was an important way of life in China until the Communist Revolution in 1945.

A 19th-century engraving of Confucius

Confucian temples usually do not have any statues. Instead, they are covered by tablets inscribed with the names of the ancestors of the people who worship in the temple. This combines the ancient Chinese tradition of ancestor worship with Confucius's teaching of the importance of or respect for the elderly.

The Jade Mummies

The ancient Egyptians often gilded mummies (covered them in gold), but only after they removed the internal organs and wrapped the bodies in cloth. More than 2,000 years ago, the ancient Chinese thought that simply covering a dead body with jade, a type of stone, would be enough to preserve it.

During the Han dynasty (206 B.C–220 A.D.), important people were sometimes buried wearing jade suits from head to toe. Jade was believed to have spiritual properties that preserved the body and made the wearer immortal.

In 1968, archaeologists uncovered two looted tombs from the Han dynasty. One tomb held the body of Prince Liu Sheng. The prince's body had decayed, and the jade suit had collapsed on him. Excavators calculated that the duds for the dead Liu Sheng were made of 2,498 jade pieces, carefully shaped to fit different parts of his body. The jade pieces were held together with more than two pounds of gold thread—quite an expensive suit!

Chinese Mythology

The Chinese also have a rich tradition of mythology. Beginning in the 3rd century A.D., Chinese writers invented many stories about gods, heroes, and ghosts. One favorite Chinese myth tells the story of the creation of the world by the god Pan Gu. In the beginning, the universe was like an egg, and inside the egg was chaos, or a state of confusion. One day, after sleeping inside the egg for 18,000 years, Pan Gu woke up and cracked the egg. By separating the light parts from the heavy parts he created the heavens and Earth. After Pan Gu died, his breath became the wind and the clouds, his voice became thunder, and one eye became the sun and the other the moon.

Another myth tells the story of the creation of people. After Pan Gu's death, Ni Wo, a goddess with a snake's body and a human's face, was born. Ni Wo was lonely, so she created people to keep her company. Ni Wo discovered that the gods of fire and water were fighting each other and destroying the earth, which was home for her new creations. Ni Wo repaired the damage they had done, saving the earth and her people. The Chinese people think of Ni Wo as their mythological mother.

Bronze figure of Guanyin, the Buddhist goddess of mercy. The goddess is sitting on a lotus flower and holds a rabbit, while a raven perches on her head.

Buddhism

In the 1st century A.D., a new religion called Buddhism came to China from India. Siddhartha Gautama, an Indian prince who had lived at the same time as Confucius, founded Buddhism. This religion teaches that through Zen (meditation) and by following the Eightfold Path, a system of guidelines similar to the Ten Commandments, Buddhists can achieve Nirvana, or peace of the spirit.

Buddhism is a more conventional religion than either Taoism or Confucianism. Buddhists go to services, practice rituals, and give money to their local temple. During the time of the Han dynasty (206 B.C.–220 A.D.), Buddhism became popular and its priests and temples wealthy and powerful. But during the Tang dynasty (618–907 A.D.), when the Buddhist priests were at the height of their power, the Tang emperors felt threatened by them and persecuted both the leaders and followers of Buddhism. However, Buddhism survived and became another influential system of thought in the development of Chinese culture.

Golden statues of Buddha adorn a Chinese temple.

Taoism

Developed in the 6th century B.C. by the philosopher Lao-tzu, Taoism is a belief system based on the harmony of man with nature. The word *tao* in Chinese means "way," and the philosophy of Taoism is based on the understanding of the proper way of life.

Many people are familiar with the most famous symbol of Taoism, the Yin and Yang. This simple form symbolizes the basic teaching of Taoism that everything in the world exists because of the interaction of opposite forces—male and female, positive and negative, hot and cold, light and dark, heaven and Earth, and good and evil. Taoism teaches that understanding these opposites promotes a life of inner peace and harmony. Like Confucianism, Taoism greatly influenced the development of Chinese society for many thousands of years.

Above: The Yin and Yang, a symbol of harmony in Chinese philosophy.
Below: An 18th-century Chinese watercolor of the philosopher Lao-tzu on his water buffalo, followed by a disciple

Christianity and Islam

Two other foreign religions also have a place in Chinese history. Islam traveled to China in 652 A.D., soon after its foundation in the Middle East. Christianity did not arrive in China until the 17th century when Jesuit Catholic missionaries from Europe came to convert the Chinese. Protestant missionaries also came to China in the 19th century. These Western missionaries found it very difficult to convert the Chinese to Christianity since the religion was associated with Western imperialism that had brought war and defeat to the Chinese. Probably the most famous missionary to come to China was Sun Yat-sen, the founding father of Taiwan, in the beginning of the 20th century.

Dr. Sun Yat-sen in an early 20th-century photograph

Above: The Great Mosque, or Qing Zhen Si, located in Xian, China. Below: A 19th-century photograph of girls from the Missionary Society Girls' Boarding School in the town of Fuzhou, Fujian Province, China

爱

CHAPTER IV

The First Emperor

In the thousands of years before China became a unified country, its various states were ruled by a succession of family dynasties and plagued by constant fighting. Qin was one of those states. This territory is in the Wei River Valley in the western part of China. Qin was small but quite wealthy because it was a thoroughfare for trade between the rest of China and the tribal lands in Central Asia.

Around 315 B.C., Qin began winning wars against some of its neighboring states, accumulating a lot of power for the Qin king. In 246 B.C., the king's 13-year-old son, Ying Zheng, inherited the throne. Zheng ruled Qin for 16 years before he began a 9-year campaign to defeat the six other Chinese states that had been at war with one another for 254 years. In 221 B.C., the victorious Zheng, who changed his name to Shihuangdi, declared himself the "First Emperor" and created a unified China. In fact, Qin was sometimes called Ch'in, which is probably where the name China originated.

Right: An engraving of the emperor Shihuangdi. Below: The terra-cotta army, Tomb of Shihuangdi, Qin dynasty (210 B.C.)

Unites China

Who was Shihuangdi?

As Emperor of China, Shihuangdi had many notable achievements. Shihuangdi was so hardworking that he set daily goals of administrative tasks for himself and would not rest until he had completed them. Under his rule, China developed one system of language, writing, currency, transportation, and weights and measures for the entire country. He spread the right of the Chinese people to buy and sell land, which increased his revenues from taxation.

Shihuangdi was also responsible for massive public works projects. He expanded canals for irrigation and transportation, and he interconnected his empire through a vast system of highways. He built magnificent public buildings in his capital, great palaces for himself, and a burial tomb, which included 6,000 soldiers made of terra-cotta clay to protect the site. Shihuangdi's most famous building project was one that joined China's many small defense walls together, then extended them into what became the Great Wall of China.

A kneeling soldier from the Tomb of Shihuangdi, Qin dynasty (210 B.C.). The soldier is shown wearing armor and ready for battle.

Despite all of these advances and progressive projects, many people in China hated Shihuangdi. The nobility disliked him because they were transplanted and deprived of their power. The common people didn't like his

heavy taxation, his harsh laws, and his forcing them to work so hard on his building projects. Legend has it that Shihuangdi arrested his own mother and sentenced one of his sons to death for disobeying his laws.

Intellectuals disliked Shihuangdi because he banned all books that advocated forms of government other than the current one. The emperor burned all books except those that flattered him or dealt with his favorite topics. The story goes that he had 460 scholars killed because he suspected they disagreed with him since they followed the teachings of the ancient Chinese philosopher Confucius.

Shihuangdi liked touring his capital city in disguise at night. He also enjoyed traveling through his empire to cities, mountains, rivers, lakes, and the seashores. Once when a strong wind impeded his crossing a river, he sent 3,000 prisoners to deforest a nearby mountain that was believed to be the home of a goddess who had created the wind. Fearing assassination, Shihuangdi had secret passages throughout his great palace and slept in a different palace apartment each night.

The two-sided swords found near the terra-cotta soldiers still sparkle and are razor sharp. They had been coated with a layer of chromium, a material used to rustproof metals. The swords prove that the Chinese used chrome plating more than 2,000 years before it was developed in Europe in 1819.

Shihuangdi's Soldiers

In 1974, some farmers were digging a well at the foot of Mount Li, which is east of the city of Xi'an and a little to the east of central China. They were surprised when one of the shovels pulled up the head of a clay warrior. When they found more sculpted warriors, they called in archaeological experts to investigate. Within two years, excavations of the area uncovered one of the greatest archaeological finds in history—the terra-cotta soldiers of Qin Shihuangdi that were sculpted more than 2,200 years before.

Warriors and horses of the terra-cotta army from the Tomb of Shihuangdi, Qin dynasty (210 B.C.)

During the first excavation of the site, archaeologists found a pit the size of four football fields that contained about 6,000 life-sized soldiers made of terra-cotta, a baked clay also used throughout the centuries to make pottery. In 1976, a second

pit was discovered containing 1,400 foot soldiers and cavalry as well as the remains of 90 war chariots. A third pit held the military headquarters, where 68 officers, 4 horses, and 1 chariot were stationed.

Experts believe Shihuangdi built his terra-cotta army to protect his burial tomb and to escort him into the afterlife. Others say the emperor wanted the army as a memorial to celebrate his military victories. Whatever the reason, it took more than 700,000 people working for 40 years to build the emperor's burial complex. In the 28 years since the tomb was found, archaeologists in China have been putting the broken pieces of the soldiers back together.

The End of Shihuangdi's Rule

During his life, Shihuangdi searched for a magic potion that would enable him to live forever. But in 210 B.C., at the age of 49, Shihuangdi became sick while on one of his journeys and died. Palace nobles withheld news of his death, murdered some of Shihuangdi's top aids, and sent a forged note to his son and **heir apparent**. The note, which Shihuangdi's son thought was from his father, ordered the son to commit suicide, which he did. Then the palace nobles elevated Shihuangdi's younger son to the throne because they hoped to control him.

Some areas of China, which had been conquered by Shihuangdi, saw his death as an opportunity to break from Qin rule. Also, some intellectuals came out against Shihuangdi's younger son. Peasants decided it was a good time to challenge imperial authority, and they began killing local officials. Local leaders led the common people in rebellion, and the noble families attempted to regain their former powers by organizing their own gangs of armed men. The young Second Emperor was soon overthrown, and the Han dynasty began in 206 B.C.

The Great Wall of China outside Beijing. This section of the Wall is called the "Wild Wall," because of the steep mountain slopes upon which it travels.

爱

CHAPTER V

The Great Wall of China

Question: What is the only structure on Earth made by humans that can be seen from the moon?

Answer: There isn't one, but if you answered the Great Wall of China, you would have made a good guess. Actually, astronauts such as Neil Armstrong, the first man to step foot on the moon, have said that the Great Wall is visible while orbiting the earth.

But that's only one of the reasons why the Great Wall of China is still considered one of the world's wonders. Construction on the Great Wall began more than 2,000 years ago, and at one time was over 4,500 miles long. The Great Wall, as it stands today, snakes through the mountains of northern China for about 1,675 miles, averaging 15 to 30 feet high. The Wall extends from Shanhaiguan Pass in the East to Jiayuguan Pass in Gansu in the West. It is so long that if it were in the United States, the Great Wall would stretch from Washington, D.C., to Denver, Colorado.

The Great Wall of China is actually the connection of many long walls that were built and rebuilt by different dynasties during more than 2,000 years of Chinese history. Over the centuries, the Great Wall was built using soil, pebbles, clay, stone, reeds, and wood. Construction of the first wall began during the 4th century B.C. During the Ming dynasty (1368–1644 A.D.), most of the Great Wall that we see today was built over about a 200-year period.

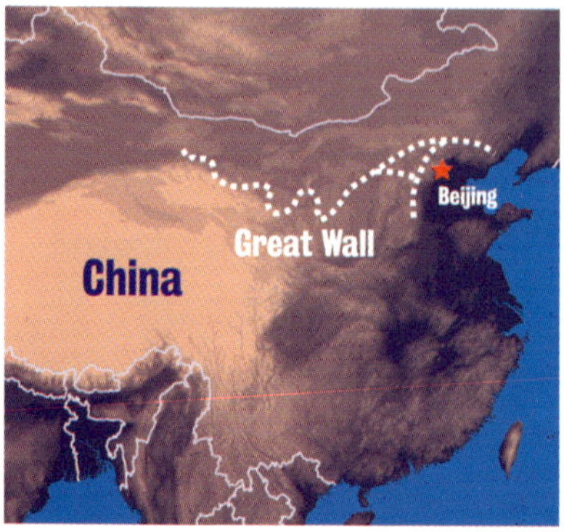

What Made the Great Wall Great?

It was during the reign of China's first Emperor, Shihuangdi, that this collection of many walls became one Great Wall. Between 221 and 207 B.C., Shihuangdi restored the ruins of older walls and linked them with new walls. The emperor wanted the Great Wall to keep in peasants, who might leave their farms to become nomads, and to keep out enemy invaders. According to historical records, the Qin section of the Wall, covering 3,000 miles, was built in 10 years, or at the rate of about 25 miles a month.

Three million people, nearly 70 percent of China's population at the time, were involved in building the Qin Wall. For every person who worked on building the Qin Great Wall, another six were needed to provide building materials and supplies. Today, experts estimate the cost of the Qin Great Wall in today's dollars at $260 billion, which would pay for roughly half of all the annual construction in the United States.

View of the Great Wall from the archway of one of the watchtowers located every few hundred feet along the wall

Another Great One

The Buddha of Leshan

The seemingly endless wall isn't the only structure in China that is considered "great." A giant statue known as the Great Buddha of Leshan is carved into the slope of Mount Emei in Sichuan Province of China. Buddha means "Enlightened One" and was applied to the Indian prince Siddhartha Gautama who founded Buddhism in the 5th century B.C.

A Buddhist monk named Haitong began carving the Buddha in 713 A.D. at the meeting point of three of China's rivers. He hoped the Buddha would protect people traveling on the dangerous rivers below.

The Great Buddha is the world's biggest Buddha at 234 feet tall and 83 feet wide at the shoulders. His head is 48 feet high, and his ears are 23 feet long. Ninety cubbyholes filled with small statues of Buddha surround the Giant Buddha, and a main temple is located near his right shoulder. The Great Buddha took 90 years to create and was finished in 803 A.D.

The Great Buddha of Leshan, Sichuan Province

During the reign of the Han dynasty (206 B.C.–220 A.D.), the poor quality of the sandy soil in the arid Gobi Desert forced Han builders to resort to an ancient and painstaking method of wall construction. First, they laid a bed of red willow reeds and twigs at the bottom of a wooden frame. Then they filled the frame with a mixture of water and fine gravel, which was tamped, or pressed, solid. When the mixture had thoroughly dried, the wooden frame was removed. This left behind a solid slab of tamped earth, strengthened by the willow reeds just as modern concrete is reinforced by steel rods.

The Han also added beacon towers to the Wall, spaced 15 to 30 miles apart. Columns of smoke were used to warn defenders of an attack. For example, one smoke column meant an outpost was being threatened by a force of fewer than 500 troops and two columns meant an attacking force of fewer than 3,000. The Han found the beacon system relayed messages faster than a rider could on a horse.

If you took all the bricks from the Ming portion of the Wall alone, they could circle the earth at the equator in a wall five feet high and three feet thick.

The Greatest Great Wall Builders

The greatest of all Great Wall builders were the Ming, who reigned in China from 1368 to 1644 A.D. The Ming built more of the Wall than any other dynasty. Their contribution was also bigger, more decorative, and more imposing than the work of previous builders. The Ming wall snakes across some of China's most difficult terrain, rising in places at an angle of 70 degrees.

The Ming relied on advanced brick-making technology to build their sections of the wall. At a time when European builders were still relying on cumbersome cut stone, the Ming used state-of-the-art kilns to mass-produce bricks, which were as strong as modern-day masonry blocks. The Ming also redesigned the wall's watchtowers and mounted modern cannons in strategic areas.

The Great Wall has always served China well. Throughout the centuries, Chinese armies were stationed along the length of the Wall to provide early warnings of invasion and a first line of defense. Great piles of straw and animal dung, which were used to build signal fires, have been found during archaeological excavations near the wall. Only when a dynasty had weakened from within were invaders from the North able to advance and conquer.

Both the Mongols (between the 13th and 14th centuries A.D.) and the Manchurians (from 1644 to 1911 A.D.) were able take power, not because of weakness in the Wall, but because of weakness in the Chinese government and the poverty of the people. The invaders took advantage of rebellion from within China and took power without having extended wars.

Above: The Great Wall of China is visible as a bright red line in this photo taken from the space shuttle Endeavour on April 10, 1994. Right: Today the Great Wall is a popular destination for tourists from China and around the world. Recently parts of the Wall have been restored.

爱

CHAPTER VI

Incredible Inventors

What do silk, tea, gunpowder, and paper have in common? The incredibly creative people of ancient China invented them all.

Smooth as Silk

One of China's first important contributions to the advancement of human civilization occurred more than 4,500 years ago with their invention of silk. A famous story tells how around 2640 B.C., the Chinese Empress Hsi Ling-Shi dropped a silkworm cocoon into her cup of tea. When she tried to pull it out, the cocoon came out as a single thread, creating the first silk used to make fine clothes. The story may be more fiction than fact, but by the year 1300 B.C., the Chinese had proven themselves very skilled at creating beautiful and expensive silk.

This 19th-century colored engraving shows silk makers boiling the cocoons to loosen the silk fibers before the silk is spun into thread.

The silk-making process involved softening silkworm cocoons in boiling water and then twisting the filaments of several cocoons together to make a very strong thread for weaving into fabrics. This impressive invention was important in Chinese history and the development of trade. From the 2nd century B.C. on, silk was exported from China to the Roman Empire in the West, linking two great civilizations. This opened the trade route between China and the Mediterranean that was called the Silk Road.

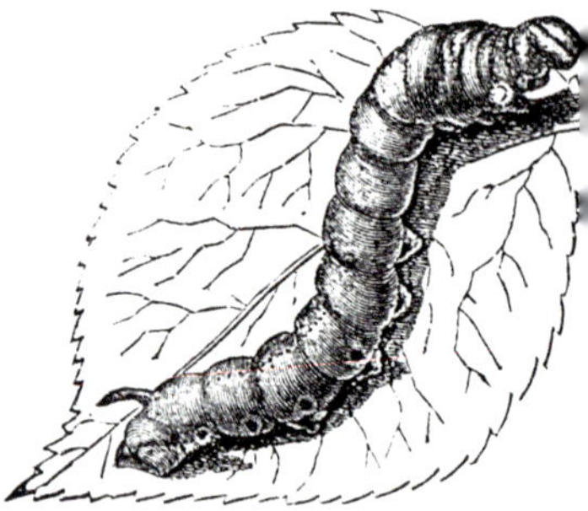

A silkworm eating a mulberry leaf, its favorite food

Tea and Gunpowder

Tea drinking began in China sometime in the 2nd century A.D., and it soon became popular, especially during the Tang dynasty (618–906 A.D.). But cutting up tea leaves by hand was time-consuming. So Chinese inventors created a mechanical tea shredder with a sharp wheel to shred the tea leaves in a fraction of the time. Tea drinking soon spread all over the world, both over the land route from Northern China and across the sea from Fukien Province on China's coast. Just think, without the Chinese, there might never have been a Boston Tea Party.

A 19th-century view of different stages in the production of tea. In the back, men dry and sort the leaves, while merchants at the front prepare to sell the tea.

It's China...from China

One of the best-known Chinese inventions is a type of pottery called porcelain. This extraordinary pottery may have been invented as early as 300 A.D. and was certainly in use by the 9th century A.D. By using secret ingredients, the Chinese made porcelain that was both beautiful and durable as well as admired and treasured. For centuries, Chinese porcelain was exported throughout the world, just as silk and tea had been before it. It was not until 1709 that the secret to making porcelain was discovered in the West.

A Ming dynasty porcelain tray, around 1780 A.D.

The fighting of wars over the last 1,200 years might have been completely different had the Chinese not invented gunpowder in about 800 A.D. Chinese scientists found that they could create an explosion by combining sulphur, charcoal, and saltpeter and then setting it on fire. Immediate military uses for this new invention included rockets launched from bamboo shoots and bamboo bombs filled with gunpowder.

Gunpowder probably came to Europe for the first time during the Mongol expansion of 1200–1300 A.D. The Europeans quickly developed the cannon and used gunpowder to fire cannonballs in wars and battles after this time. But the Chinese also had a festive use for their new invention. In addition to weapons, they used gunpowder to make the first fireworks.

Fireworks (above) and the abacus (below) are just two of the many technological advances made by the Chinese.

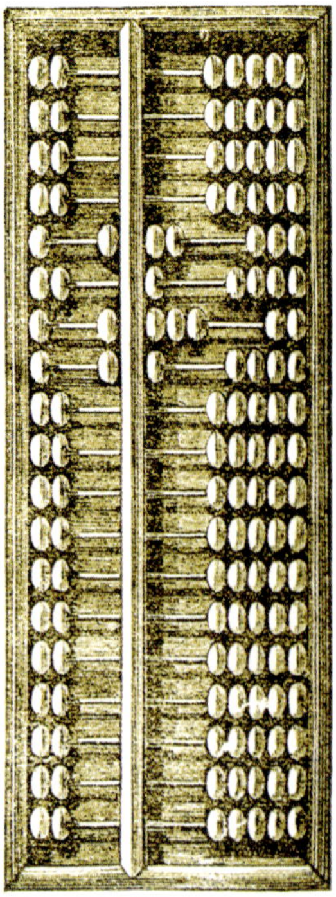

Technological Advances

The Chinese made many other great contributions to the advancement of science and technology. By the 3rd century A.D., Chinese scientists had learned to make magnets. They would heat pieces of metal to red-hot temperatures and then allow the metal to cool in a north/south position. They placed these magnets on a piece of reed. Then by floating the magnets in a bowl of water marked with directions for north, south, east, and west, the Chinese created the first compasses. By the 11th century A.D., compasses were being used to navigate Chinese ships.

China suffers many earthquakes, and so the country's scientists developed the world's first seismograph, a device for detecting earthquakes. They also created the world's first device for counting, called the *abacus*, and used wine as an anaesthetic as early as the 3rd century A.D.

Paper and Printing

Although legend says that the first paper was given to the Chinese emperor in 105 A.D., archaeological evidence tells us that paper was actually in use about 200 years before this. The Chinese made high-quality and relatively inexpensive paper from bark, bamboo, and hemp. Sometimes paper was made from cloth and silk fibers, which were softened, boiled, and washed to make pulp and then rolled into sheets and allowed to dry.

So what did the Chinese do with all of this paper? Using an elaborate system of writing and lots of ingenuity, the Chinese made the first known printed book in 868 A.D. Almost 200 years later, they developed moveable type, which allowed them to begin printing many more books. The use of paper and printing also led to the invention of playing cards and even paper money, which the Chinese introduced into Europe in the 10th century A.D. Before that time, all money had been coins.

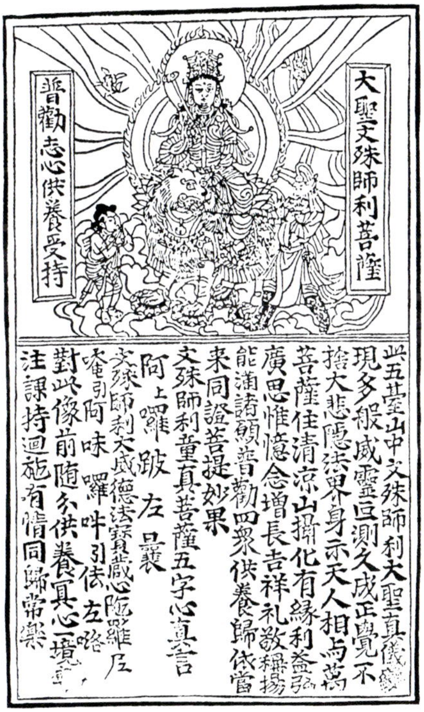

A 10th-century Buddhist printed text made from a woodcut

An assistant (center) prepares ink for two poets in this ancient Chinese watercolor.

Among some other Chinese inventions were folding umbrellas, kites, fans, and wallpaper. They also developed some of our most popular foods, such as peaches, apricots, lemons, and oranges. Many people believe that the ancient Chinese invented spaghetti.

A bronze statue of a stork stands outside the Hall of Supreme Harmony in the Forbidden City, Beijing.

A Great Civilization

China is home to the world's longest continuous civilization. What began as a small group of farming villages is now a nation that covers more than 3.5 million square miles and has a population of 1.2 billion people. On this tour you've learned a little about China's history, its culture, and the great contributions the Chinese people have made to the world. Although China has been a relatively closed society since the Communist Revolution in 1949, in recent years it has begun to open its doors to the world, allowing us to learn more about this ancient and fascinating culture.

Glossary

artisan person who works at a trade requiring skill with the hands

Buddhism religion that seeks peace through meditation and prayer

Confucianism philosophy that teaches the importance of centralized authority

divination art of telling the future by interpreting omens and signs

dynasty ruling family that passes control from one member to the next

Eurasia landmass that includes the continents of Europe and Asia

feudal state system of government where the people agree to serve a landowner in return for protection and land to farm

heir apparent person with legal claim to a title or throne when the current ruler dies

Huns nomadic people who originated in north-central Asia and invaded China in the 3rd century B.C.

irrigation act of supplying land with water by artificial means

legacy something left after one dies

Mohism philosphy that teaches a message of love and compassion

Mongols powerful group of warriors who conquered the Chinese in 1278 A.D.

mythology stories about gods and heroes that reveal the worldview of a people

nomad person with no fixed home who moves according to the season, hunting and searching for food and water

porcelain type of pottery developed by the Chinese in the 4th century A.D.

Taoism belief system based on the harmony of mankind with nature

terrace raised embankment with a leveled top, used in farming mountainous areas

INDEX